Studies of Torah Volume one

The Torah

The Torah is the first five books of the Tanak: Genesis (B' RESHEET), Exodus (SH' MOT), Leviticus (VAYIKRA), Numbers (B' MIDBAR), and Deuteronomy (D' VARIM). All five were written by Moses who was inspired by the Holy Spirit.

The word "Torah" in Hebrew means: "utterance, teaching, instruction or revelation from Elohim." It comes from "horah" which means: "to direct, to teach" and derives from the stem "yara" which means: "to shoot or throw." Therefore, there are two aspects to the word Torah: 1) aiming or pointing in the right direction, and 2) movement in that direction. It is extremely misunderstood by many because it is often improperly translated as "The Law." Rather, the Torah is the Ketubah - The Wedding Contract.

Israel is a bride redeemed from slavery. It was a free gift. Lives were spared because of the Blood of the Lamb (Yeshua) on the doorpost. Israel consisted of anyone who wanted to follow the Elohim of Israel (referred to as the mixed multitude or EREB RAB). Israel has always been interwoven with the nations.

Once the mixed multitude was delivered from slavery, they were then given the option to accept the Torah.

The assembling at Sinai was a wedding ceremony.

Moses came, summoned the leaders of the people, and present them with all these words which YHWH had ordered Him to say. All the people answered as one, Everything YHWH has said, we will do." Moses reported the words of the people to YHWH. - Exodus 19:7-9

This is the day we said, "I do."

There are many who proclaim that the Torah, which they call "the Law," was too difficult for Israel to obey. This is simply untrue. Elohim was not putting on Israel a yoke of slavery. He was, after all, freeing them from slavery. Our freedom included with it the instructions for a better way of life.

After detailing the blessings and curses to Yisrael, Moses specifically stated:

Now what I am commanding you today is not too difficult for you or beyond your reach. It is not up in heaven, so that you have to ask, 'Who will ascend into heaven to get it and proclaim it to us so we may obey it? Nor is it beyond the sea, so that you have to ask, 'Who will cross the sea to get it and proclaim it to us so we may obey it? No, the Word is very near you, for it is in your mouth and in your heart so you may obey it." - Deuteronomy 30:11-14

Here is how we know that we love Elohim's children: when we love Elohim, we also do what He commands. For loving Elohim means obeying His commands. Moreover, His commands are not burdensome, because everything which has Elohim as its Father overcomes the world. And this is what victoriously overcomes the world: our trust. - 1 John 5:2-4

1. How many books are in the Torah?

_____

_____

_____

2. List the names of the books that are in the Torah (both the English names and the Hebrew names)

_____

_____

_____

3. What does the word "Torah" mean?

_____

_____

_____

4. What are the two aspects to the word "Torah"?

_____

_____

_____

5. What Scripture describes our answer to the wedding proposal?

_____

_____

_____

6. Describe the meaning of the Hebrew term EREB RAB

_____

_____

_____

7. Finish the sentence: When we love Elohim, we also

_____

_____

_____

8. Does Elohim consider the Torah to be a yoke of slavery? Explain your answer.

_____

_____

_____

9. What is the Ketubah?

_____

_____

_____

10. Whose blood did the blood of the Lamb represent, which the Israelites put on their doorpost?

_____

_____

_____

Seek the Kingdom First

And this is the confidence that we have in Him, that, if we ask anything according to His will, He hears us; And if we know that He hears us, whatsoever we ask, we know that we have the petitions that we desired of Him. – 1 John 5:14-15

This is an essential Scripture in understanding your relationship with Elohim. When you read this Scripture closely what you'll see is that – as a result of this – we are assured that Elohim hears us… when we submit to Him. When we shut down what we want and instead ask Elohim for His will, it shows that we trust Him.

So now, we have an understanding with Elohim. He says: "When you ask My will to be done, I hear you." So now watch after you pray. Understand that what will now transpire will be according to His plan for your life. We know that His will is His word (John 1:1-3, 14). Through the Messiah Yeshua Elohim dwells with people (2 Cor 6:16; John 14:23).

You will know Elohim's answer because it will line up with His word.

Wherefore the rather, brethren, give diligence to make your calling and election sure: for if you do these things, you shall never fall: For so an entrance shall be ministered unto you abundantly into the everlasting Kingdom of our Lord and Saviour Yeshua. – 2Peter 1:10-11

We were made for Elohim's pleasure (Eph 1:4-5). He is the potter; you are the clay (Isaiah 45:9; Isaiah 64:8).

Read the following Scriptures:

John 15:19
Matthew 22:1-14
Ephesians 1:4-5
Isaiah 45:9
Isaiah 64:8
1 Peter 1:13-21
Matthew 6:25-33

We see through Ephesians 1:4-5 and 1 Peter 1:13-21 that we were chosen (Elohim's set apart people) before the foundation of the world. Based on what Elohim foreknew about us, He pre-destined.

1. Why is the 1 John 5:14-15 scripture important to your relationship with Elohim?

   _____

   _____

   _____

2. What is the understanding you now have with Elohim, as a result of 1 John 5:14-15?

   _____

   _____

   _____

3. Read the following scriptures: Matt. 26:41; Matt. 13:33; Mark 14:38; Luke 21:36. What do these scriptures all have in common?

   _____

   _____

   _____

4. How will we know for sure if the answer to what Elohim's will is-given a certain situation-is really Elohim's answer? How do we check it? What is our guide?

_____

_____

_____

5. Read Proverbs 3:5-6. Based on this scripture why is it important to shut down what we want and ask His will regarding a situation?

_____

_____

_____

6. Based on 2 Peter 1:10-11, why do we want to make our calling and election sure?

_____

_____

_____

7. What do 2 Peter 1:10-11 and Matthew 6:25-33 have in common? How are these scriptures similar?

_____

_____

_____

8. After reading Matthew 22:1-14, How did the people respond to the wedding invitation? How does it relate to Elohim's calling on a person's life?

_____

_____

_____

Who is your neighbor?

An expert in Torah stood up to try and trap him by asking, "Rabbi, what should I do to obtain eternal life?" But Yeshua said to him, "What is written in the Torah? How do you read it?" He answered, "You are to love YHWH your Elohim with all your heart, with all your soul, with all your strength and with all your understanding, and your neighbor as yourself." "That's the right answer," Yeshua said. "Do this, and you will have life."

But he, wanting to justify himself, said to Yeshua, "And who is my 'neighbor'?" Taking up the question, Yeshua said: "A man was going down from Yerushalayim to Yericho when he was attacked by robbers. They stripped him naked and beat him up, then went off, leaving him half dead. By coincidence, a cohen was going down on that road, but when he saw him, he passed by on the other side.

But a man from Shomron who was traveling came upon him, and when he saw him, he was moved with compassion. So, he went up to him, put oil and wine on his wounds and bandaged them. Then he set him on his own donkey, brought him to an inn and took care of him. The next day, he took out two days' wages, gave them to the innkeeper and said, 'Look after him, and if you spend more than this, I'll pay you back when I return.' Of these three, which one seems to you to have become the 'neighbor' of the man who fell among robbers?" He answered, "The one who showed mercy toward him." Yeshua said to him, "You go and do as he did." - Luke 10:25-37

For He will rescue the needy when they cry, the poor too and those with none to help them. He will have pity on the poor and needy, and the lives of the needy He will save. He will redeem them from oppression and violence, their blood will be precious in his view. - Psalm 72:12-14

But the needy he raises up from their distress and increases their families like sheep. When the upright see this, they rejoice, while the wicked are reduced to silence. Let whoever is wise observe these things and consider YHWH's loving deeds. - Psalm 107:41-43

We can see from these Scriptures your "neighbor" has nothing to do with proximity. Rather, YHWH considers your "neighbor" to be the needy, the downtrodden, the afflicted. Can you think of someone in your life who is oppressed, picked on, put down on... maybe people want to beat him up. Maybe you are the one Elohim is trusting to show mercy toward him.

Based on the Scriptures given in this chapter, answer the following questions:

1. Who is your neighbor?

_____
_____
_____

2. What can you do to show mercy to this neighbor?

_____
_____
_____

3. How did the man answer when Yeshua asked him "What is written in the Torah? How do you read it?"

_____

_____

_____

4. Read Matthew 5:7 and explain how this Scripture relates to Yeshua's story in Luke 10:25-37

_____

_____

_____

5. Read Proverbs 3:27-30. Explain how this passage of Scripture relates to what we have covered in this chapter.

_____

_____

_____

The measure you use

Yeshua said that each person will be measured with the measure he uses:

Show compassion, just as your Father shows compassion.

"Don't judge, and you won't be judged. Don't condemn, and you won't be condemned.

"Forgive, and you will be forgiven. Give, and you will receive gifts -- the full measure, compacted, shaken together and overflowing, will be put right in your lap. For the measure with which you measure out will be used to measure back to you!" - Luke 6:36-38

Consider for a moment how David was measured by the measure he used.

ADONAI sent Natan to David. He came and said to him, "In a certain city there were two men, one rich, the other poor.

The rich man had vast flocks and herds; but the poor man had nothing, except for one little ewe lamb, which he had bought and reared. It had grown up with him and his children; it ate from his plate, drank from his cup, lay on his chest - it was like a daughter to him.

One day a traveler visited the rich man, and instead of picking an animal from his own flock or herd to cook for his visitor, he took the poor man's lamb and cooked it for the man who had come to him."

David exploded with anger against the man and said to Natan, "As ADONAI lives, the man who did this deserves to die!

For doing such a thing, he has to pay back four times the value of the lamb - and also because he had no pity."

Natan said to David, "You are the man. "Here is what ADONAI, the Elohim of Isra'el says: 'I anointed you king over Isra'el. I rescued you from the power of Sha'ul.

I gave you your master's house and your master's wives to embrace. I gave you the house of Isra'el and the house of Y'hudah. And if that had been too little, I would have added to you a lot more.

"'So why have you shown such contempt for the word of ADONAI and done what I see as evil? You murdered Uriyah the Hitti with the sword and taken his wife as your own wife; you put him to death with the sword of the people of 'Amon.

Now therefore, the sword will never leave your house - because you have shown contempt for me and taken the wife of Uriyah the Hitti as your own wife.'

Here is what ADONAI says: 'I will generate evil against you out of your own household. I will take your wives before your very eyes and give them to your neighbor; he will go to bed with your wives, and everyone will know about it.

For you did it secretly, but I will do this before all Isra'el in broad daylight.'"

David said to Natan, "I have sinned against ADONAI." Natan said to David, "ADONAI also has taken away your sin. You will not die. -2 Samuel 12:1-13

Consider the following before you measure.

Finally, all of you, be one in mind and feeling; love as brothers; and be compassionate and humble-

minded, not repaying evil with evil or insult with insult, but, on the contrary, with blessing. For it is to this that you have been called, so that you may receive a blessing.

For "Whoever wants to love life and see good days must keep his tongue from evil and his lips from speaking deceit, turn from evil and do good, seek peace and chase after it.

For ADONAI keeps his eyes on the righteous, and his ears are open to their prayers; but the face of ADONAI is against those who do evil things."

For who will hurt you if you become zealots for what is good?

But even if you do suffer for being righteous, you are blessed! Moreover, don't fear what they fear or be disturbed, but treat the Messiah as holy, as Lord in your hearts; while remaining always ready to give a reasoned answer to anyone who asks you to explain the hope you have in you - yet with humility and fear, keeping your conscience clear, so that when you are spoken against, those who abuse the good behavior flowing from your union with the Messiah may be put to shame.

For if Elohim has in fact willed that you should suffer, it is better that you suffer for doing what is good than for doing what is evil. - 1 Peter 3:8-17

Answer the following questions:

1. How was David measured by the measure he used in his sin against Elohim?

_____

_____

_____

2. What happens when we judge?

_____

_____

_____

3. According to 1 Peter, why is it important to keep your conscience clear?

_____

_____

_____

Then Kefa came up and said to him, "Rabbi, how often can my brother sin against me and I have to forgive him? As many as seven times?" "No, not seven times," answered Yeshua, "but seventy times seven! Because of this, the Kingdom of Heaven may be compared with a king who decided to settle accounts with his deputies. Right away they brought forward a man who owed him many millions; and since he couldn't pay, his master ordered that he, his wife, his children and all his possessions be sold to pay the debt. But the servant fell down before him. 'Be patient with me,' he begged, 'and I will pay back everything.' So out of pity for him, the master let him go and forgave the debt.

"But as that servant was leaving, he came upon one of his fellow servants who owed him some tiny sum. He grabbed him and began to choke him, crying, 'Pay back what you owe me! 'His fellow servant fell before him and begged, 'Be patient with me, and I will pay you back.' But he refused; instead, he had him thrown in jail until he should repay the debt. When the other servants saw what had happened, they were extremely distressed; and they went and told their master everything that had taken place. Then the master summoned his servant and said, 'You wicked servant! I forgave you all that debt just because you begged me to do it. Shouldn't you have had pity on your fellow servant, just as I had pity on you?' And in anger his master turned him over to the jailers for punishment until he paid back everything he owed. This is how my heavenly Father will treat you, unless you each forgive your brother from your hearts." -Matthew 18:21-35

4. Based on Matthew 18:21-35, how was the servant measured by the measure he used - in regard to his fellow servant?

_____

_____

_____

5. Sum up in your own words what Yeshua is saying in Matthew 18:35?

_____

_____

_____

We wrestle not against flesh and blood

Use all the armor and weaponry that Elohim provides, so that you will be able to stand against the deceptive tactics of the Adversary.

For we are not struggling against human beings, but against the rulers, authorities and cosmic powers governing this darkness, against the spiritual forces of evil in the heavenly realm. - Ephesians 6:11-12

We know that there is a war in heaven. We are part of a spiritual war whether we choose to participate in this war or not. We are not battling against flesh and blood but against spirits.

Then Elohim said, "Let us make humankind in our image, in the likeness of ourselves; and let them rule over the fish in the sea, the birds in the air, the animals, and over all the earth, and over every crawling creature that crawls on the earth." - Genesis 1:26

Man was given dominion over the earth and only a man has authority on the earth.

Don't you know that you people are Elohim's temple and that Elohim's Spirit lives in you? So, if anyone destroys Elohim's temple, Elohim will destroy him. For Elohim's temple is holy, and you yourselves are that temple.

- 1 Corinthians 3:16-17

You have been built on the foundation of the emissaries and the prophets, with the cornerstone being Yeshua the Messiah himself. In union with him the whole building is held together, and it is growing into a holy temple in union with the Lord. Yes, in union with him, you yourselves are being built together into a spiritual dwelling-place for Elohim! - Ephesians 2:20-22

An evil spirit cannot violate your will.

Therefore, submit to Elohim. Moreover, take a stand against the Adversary, and he will flee from you.

- James 4:7

If we submit to Elohim and resist the devil, he will flee. Since evil spirits cannot violate our will they must have us in agreement with them in order for them to take possession of us. Once we become their host, they now have the authority that we were given. It is then that a demonic spirit can enact whatever plan they have - through us.

"Or again, how can someone break into a strong man's house and make off with his possessions unless he first ties up the strong man? After that he can ransack his house. - Matthew 12:29

A man is slave to whatever has mastered him (2 Peter 2:19).

A man can have many demons in him at one time.

They sailed on and landed in the region of the Gerasenes, which is opposite the Galil. As Yeshua stepped ashore, a man from the town who had demons came to meet him. For a long time he had not worn clothes; and he lived, not in a house, but in the burial caves.

Catching sight of Yeshua, he screamed, fell down in front of him and yelled, "Yeshua! Son of Elohim Ha'Elyon! What do you want with me? I beg you, don't torture me!" For Yeshua had ordered the unclean spirit to come out of the man. It had often taken hold of him — he had been kept under guard, chained hand and foot, but had broken the bonds and been driven by the demon into the desert. Yeshua asked him, "What is your name?" "Legion," he said, because many demons had entered him. They begged Yeshua not to order them to go off into the Bottomless Pit. - Luke 8:26-31

We know that LEGION is a Roman word which means 6,826 soldiers. So - in essence - this man had 6,826 soldiers. Each demon has its own specialty, and they work together to gain possession of a host. Example: spirit of pride, spirit of suicide, spirit of greed, spirit of heaviness, spirit of the anti-messiah, etc. etc. Imagine 6,826 evil spirits.

How do they bind a strong man and use him as their human host?

They tempt us with even imagination.

No one being tempted should say, "I am being tempted by Elohim." For Elohim cannot be tempted by evil, and Elohim himself tempts no one. Rather, each person is being tempted whenever he is being dragged off and enticed by the bait of his own desire. Then, having conceived, the desire gives birth to sin; and when sin is fully grown, it gives birth to death. - James 1:13-15

So rid yourselves of all vulgarity and obvious evil and receive meekly the Word implanted in you that can save your lives. - James 1:21

Again, they cannot violate our will. Elohim tests, the devil tempts. They give us evil imaginations, trying to hook us. We always have a choice.

No temptation has seized you beyond what people normally experience, and Elohim can be trusted not to allow you to be tempted beyond what you can bear. On the contrary, along with the temptation he will also provide the way out, so that you will be able to endure. - 1 Corinthians 10:13

Elohim will always give us a way out of the temptation (another option to consider which is in accordance with His Word). Every day we are given a choice: to eat from the tree He told us not to eat from or to eat from the tree of life. If we give into the temptation of the devil, he will then have control of our house. We have then surrendered our Elohim-given authority (GEN 1:26), our own dominion.

"When an unclean spirit comes out of a person, it travels through dry country seeking rest and does not find it. 44 Then it says to itself, 'I will return to the house I left.' When it arrives, it finds the house standing empty, swept clean and put in order. 45 Then it goes and takes with it seven other spirits more evil than itself, and they come and live there — so that in the end, the person is worse off than he was before. This is how it will be for this wicked generation." - Matthew 12:43-45

Each time we come to our senses and begin to refuse to entertain the spirit's ideas, it will immediately seek ways to get its host back. It will go get reinforcements (more evil spirits) to try to regain you as a host.

Answer the following questions:

1. Explain Genesis 1:26 and why man has authority on the earth.

_____

_____

_____

2. How does a spirit attempt to hijack your dominion?

_____

_____

_____

3. Explain why we wrestle not against flesh and blood.

_____

_____

_____

4. How do we prevent evil spirits from using us as their human host?

_____

_____

_____

5. What does it mean to bind a strong man's house? How does a spirit do this?

_____

_____

_____

6. How many demons are in a legion?

_____

_____

_____

7. In order to submit to Elohim, we must do what?

_____

_____

_____

Yeshua came for sinners

And when the scribes and Pharisees saw Him eating with the tax collectors and sinners, they said to His disciples, ''Why does He eat and drink with tax collectors and sinners?'' And hearing this, Yeshua said to them, 'Those who are strong have no need of a physician, but those who are sick. I did not come to call the righteous to repentance, but sinners.'' - Mark 2:16-17

Yeshua came for sinners.

If I have to boast, I shall boast of matters that show my weakness. - 2 Corinthians 11:30

Of such a one I shall boast, but of myself I shall not boast, except in my weaknesses. - 2 Corinthians 12:5

And He said to me, ''My grace is sufficient for you, for My power is perfected in weakness.'' Most gladly, then, I shall rather boast in my weaknesses, so that the power of Mashiach rests on me. Therefore I take pleasure in weaknesses, in insults, in needs, in persecutions, in distresses, for the sake of Mashiach. For when I am weak, then I am strong. - 2 Corinthians 12:9-10

It is our infirmities that qualify us for His mighty power to work in our lives.

And passing by, He saw a man, blind from birth. And His disciples asked Him, saying, ''Rabbi, who sinned, this man or his parents, that he should be born blind?'' Yeshua answered, ''Neither this man nor his parents sinned, but that the works of Elohim might be made manifest in Him.'' - John 9:1-3

As long as we deal with our struggles in a way that is pleasing to YHWH we know it is all going to work out.

So then, those suffering according to the desire of Elohim should commit their lives to a trustworthy Creator, in doing good. - 1 Peter 4:19

This baptism of fire will circumcise our hearts, removing our impurities.

Beloved ones, do not be surprised at the fiery trial that is coming upon you, to try you, as though some unusual matter has befallen you, but as you share Mashiach's sufferings, rejoice exultingly at the revelation of His esteem. - 1 Peter 4:12-13

You suffer with Him, you reign with Him.

If we endure, we shall also reign with Him. If we deny, He also shall deny us. - 2 Timothy 2:12

YHWH is in the timing. When the time is right, He makes His deliverance known.

The end of a matter is better than its beginning, and patience is better than pride. - Ecclesiastes 7:8

It is better to go to the house of mourning than to go to the house of feasting, for that is the end of all man. And the living take it to heart. Sorrow is better than laughter, for by the sadness of the face the heart becomes better. The heart of the wise is in the house of mourning, but the heart of fools is in the house of rejoicing. - Ecclesiastes 7:2-4

YHWH is rich in mercy. He can afford your sin.

In order to make known the riches of his glory for vessels of mercy, which he has prepared beforehand for glory - Romans 9:23

And He himself is an atoning offering for our sins, and not for ours only but also for all the world. - 1 John 2:2

He will meet you where you're at but He's not gonna let you stay there forever.

The one who says he stays in Him ought Himself also to walk, even as He walked. - 1 John 2:6

To repent is to turn away.

Turn away from evil and do good, seek peace, and pursue it. - Psalms 34:14

32

The reverence of YHWH is the beginning of wisdom, and the knowledge of the Set Apart One is understanding. - Proverbs 9:10

And He said to man, 'See, the reverence of YHWH, that is wisdom, and to turn from evil is understanding. - Job 28:28

A repentant heart helps us to stay on track.

''Two men went up to the Temple to pray - the one a Pharisee and the other a tax collector. The Pharisee stood and began to pray with himself this way, 'Elohim I thank You that I am not like the rest of men, swindlers, unrighteous, adulterers, or even as this tax collector. I fast twice a week, I give tithes of all that I possess.'

But the tax collector standing at a distance would not even raise his eyes to the heavens, but was beating his breast, saying, ''Elohim, show favor unto me, a sinner!'

''I say to you, this man went down to his house declared right, rather than the other. For everyone who is exalting himself shall be humbled, and he who is humbling himself shall be exalted.'' - Luke 18:10-14

Answer the following questions:

1. The scribes and Pharisees made a comment about Yeshua eating and drinking with tax collectors and sinners. What was Yeshua's response?

_____

_____

_____

2. What does it say in 2 Corinthians about our weaknesses? Why are they important?

_____

_____

_____

3. What is it that qualifies us for His mighty power to work in our lives?

_____

_____

_____

4. Finish the sentence: You suffer with Him,

_____

_____

_____

5. Why is it better to go to the house of mourning than to go to the house of feasting?

_____

_____

_____

6. *Yeshua will meet you where you're at but He's gonna let you stay there forever. Why is that?*

_____

_____

_____

7. *What does it mean to repent? What does it involve?*

_____

_____

_____

8. *In Luke 18:10-14, describe how the tax collector had a repentant heart?*

_____

_____

_____

Building

Everything which is seen came from what is unseen. It didn't come from nothing. It came from what is unseen. Wisdom was before Genesis 1:1.

Elohim brought me forth as the first of His works, before His deeds of old (Proverb 8:8).

YHWH spoke everything into existence with His Word.

Through faith, through trust, we understand that the worlds were framed by the Word of Elohim. So that the things which are seen were made not of things which do appear. - Hebrew 11:3

Everything in the physical world, originated in the spiritual realm. It is His Word which brings it across that threshold.

By the Word of YHWH the heavens were made, and all their host by the breath of His mouth. - Psalm 33:6

Hebrew is the mother tongue. It is an action language: the seed language. The seed is the Word of YHWH (an encapsulated beginning). His Word made everything seen which was unseen.

Faith is the substance of things hoped for, the evidence of things not seen. - Hebrews 11:1

We must have faith that YHWH's Word can bring anything He Wills into existence.

We are not looking on what is seen, but what is not seen. For what is seen passes away, but what is not seen is everlasting. - 2 Corinthians 4:18

There is something about the written word. Writing brings what is unseen (or spiritual) into the physical world. Once the words hit the paper, they have crossed a threshold. It's almost as if they have gone from one dimension to another. Most importantly, it is YHWH's Word, not ours which has this power.

I noticed a shift once I started writing my prayers down. The prayers we say need to be based on His Word and all of it seems to become eternal once it is written down. There is a movie I recommend watching, called "War Room." The woman of the house begins writing her prayers down along with the Scriptures those prayers are based on. Her prayers get answered. I have noticed this in my own life as well.

YHWH has answered many of my prayers throughout the years. But something I noticed; was that when I started writing them down; my communication with YHWH became even more interesting.

Moses would repeat YHWH's Word back to him.

''And now, I pray, let the power of YHWH be great, as You have spoken, saying, 'YHWH is patient and of great kindness, forgiving wickedness and transgression,

but by no means leaving unpunished; visiting the wickedness of the fathers on the children to the third and fourth generation.'

'Please forgive the wickedness of this people, according to the greatness of Your kindness, as You have forgiven this people, from Egypt even until now.''

And YHWH said, ''I shall forgive, according to your word.'' - Numbers 14:17-20

YHWH is faithful to His Word. His Word is His Will. Our prayers need to line up with His Word/His Will. Remember that His Word can create, and we are told to build on a rock rather than on sand (Luke 6:47-49).

''Truly, I say to you, whatever you bind on earth shall be bound in heaven, and whatever you loosen on earth shall be loosed in heaven. - Matthew 18:18

When Yeshua rebuked the devil in the wilderness; all three times it was with the Torah. And all three times He said ''It is Written.''

Again, we see the power of YHWH's Written Word in Daniel 5:5 (The writing is on the wall).

There are some who believe that the original Ten Commandments (the ones Moses broke on the ground) were written on stone that came straight from the throne of YHWH. Moses was away for 40 days and 40 nights and he did not eat bread or drink water. We know that a person cannot survive under these conditions. It is possible he went through some sort of time warp. Since YHWH is not subject to physical time, Moses could have been translated out of time and into the presence of YHWH (the throne room) where YHWH spoke the Words and gave him the stones with the commandments.

Remember that Mount Zion is located in the heavenly realm, another dimension. This also appears to be the dimension in which the 144,000 are located with the Lamb on the mountain in heaven.

Let us remember that YHWH establishes everything by the mouth of two or three witnesses (Matthew 18:16 - Deuteronomy 17:6 - Deuteronomy 19:15).

Remember that angels serve as witnesses also.

And you, being dead in your trespasses and the uncircumcision of your flesh, He has made alive together with Him, having forgiven you all trespasses, having blotted out the handwriting against us - by the dogmas - which stood against us. And He has taken it out of the way, having nailed it to the stake. Having stripped the principalities and the authorities, He made a public display of them, having prevailed over them in it. - Colossians 2:13-15

When Yeshua was crucified - He showed not only men, but the entire angelic population - the devil's true colors. Remember that the devil often masquerades as an angel of light.

Angels serve as witnesses to the Written Word of YHWH. By basing your prayers on the Word and writing those prayers down you are establishing them in the eyes of many (unseen) witnesses.

We too, then, having so great a cloud of witnesses all around us, let us lay aside every weight and the sin which so easily entangles us, and let us run with endurance the race put before us. - Hebrews 12:1

Finally, the most important thing to understand is that what you are asking must be Elohim's Will. If it is not Elohim's Will, you are not building on rock; you are building on sand! Elohim will not answer a prayer if it is not His Will. All the faith in the world won't help you.

Yes, indeed! I tell you that whoever trusts in me will also do the works I do! Indeed, he will do greater ones, because I am going to the Father. In fact, whatever you ask for in my name, I will do, so that the Father may be glorified in the Son. If you ask me for something in my name, I will do it. - John 14:12-14

Answer the following questions:

1. Read Matthew 7:24-27 and explain why we are building a house on the rock when we pray for things which are in accordance with Elohim's Will?

_____
_____
_____

2. What brings what is spiritual across the threshold and into the physical?

_____

_____

_____

3. Finish the sentence: What is seen passes away, but

_____

_____

_____

4. In Numbers 14:17-20 how did Moses present his prayer request to YHWH?

_____

_____

_____

5. Describe the power of Elohim's written word in Daniel 5:5.

_____

_____

_____

The Next Exodus

The next Exodus is often called 'The Greater Exodus.''

''*And I shall bring you out from the peoples and gather you out of the lands where you are scattered, with a mighty hand, and with an outstretched arm, and with wrath poured out.*

And I shall bring you into the wilderness of the peoples and shall enter into judgment with you face to face there.

As I entered into judgment with your fathers in the wilderness of the land of Egypt, so I shall enter into judgment with you, declares the Adonai YHWH.''

 - Ezekiel 20:34-36

There will be a face-to-face judgment with YHWH in the wilderness just as there was the first time. History will repeat itself.

''*Remember this and show yourselves men; turn it back, you transgressors.*

Remember the former of long ago, for I am El, and there is no one else - Elohim, and there is no one like Me,

declaring the end from the beginning, and from of old that which has not been done, saying, 'My counsel stands, and all My delight I do.' ''

 - Isaiah 46:8-10

If you want to know the end, go back to the beginning. It is all going to repeat itself: 1) Two Witnesses (only instead of Moses and Aaron) it will be two other witnesses. 2) Judgments. Only instead of ten judgments on Egypt, there will be 21 judgments (7 seals, 3 judgments each) on the whole world. 3) Exodus. Instead of an Exodus out of Egypt, this time the Exodus will be from all over the world. Just like the first time, YHWH's people will be exempt from the judgments on the world; but will be subject to the face-to-face judgments which result from not obeying the Torah, while in the wilderness.

You'll remember that during the first Exodus, the carcasses fell; of those who disobeyed the Torah. Paul (filled with The Holy Spirit) addresses the last generation. He warns us NOT TO MAKE THE SAME MISTAKES as those who journeyed through the wilderness during the FIRST EXODUS.

For I do not want you to be ignorant, brothers, that all our fathers were under the cloud, and all passed through the sea,

and all were immersed into Moses in the cloud and in the sea,

and all ate the same spiritual food,

and all drank the same spiritual drink. For they drank of that spiritual Rock that followed, and the Rock was Mashiach.

However, with most of them Elohim was not well pleased, for they were laid low in the wilderness.

And these became example for us, so that we should not list after evil, as those indeed lusted.

And do not become idolaters as some of them, as it has been written, ''The people sat down to eat and to drink, and stood up to play.''

Neither should we commit whoring, as some of them did, and in one day twenty-three thousand fell,

neither let us try Mashiach, as some of them also tried, and were destroyed by serpents,

neither grumble, as some of them also grumbled, and were destroyed by the destroyer.

AND ALL THESE CAME UPON THEM AS EXAMPLES, AND THEY WERE WRITTEN AS A WARNING TO US, ON WHOM THE ENDS OF THE AGES HAVE COME,

so that he who thinks he stands, let him take heed lest he fall.

- 1 Corinthians 10:1-12

Fairly straightforward. Don't make the same mistakes they did. Isaiah speaks to the last generation concerning the next Exodus (Greater Exodus).

Then YHWH shall create above every dwelling place of Mount Zion, and above her assemblies, a cloud and smoke by day and the shining of a flaming fire by night, for over all the esteem shall be a covering,

and a booth for shade in the daytime from the heat, for a place of refuge, and for a shelter from storm and rain.

 - Isaiah 4:5-6

A booth is a tent or tabernacle. This was written after the first Exodus and specifically points to the next Exodus. Isaiah tells us that we will once again be moving from camp to camp. When the clouds by day and fire by night moves, we move.

Beginning at Sukkot (where the first Exodus started), there were 41 camps that the Yisraelites stayed in, before they entered into the promised land (Numbers 33).

Yeshua was resurrected during the Omer count and ascended into the heavens on Day 41 of the Omer count.

Therefore, if those patterns have future meaning, we may see 41 different camps around the earth while the people are being regathered.

The Feast of Tabernacles (also called Sukkot) is when we commemorate how and when we left Egypt. It's a ''set apart rehearsal,'' our escape plan for the end. Those who have been observing this Appointed Time - as the command says (Lev 23) - know this.

''*Watch then at all times, and pray that you be counted worthy to escape all this about to take place, and to stand before the Son of Man.*'' - *Luke 21:36*

We want to be praying to be part of The Greater Exodus. Especially, those in prison. The Covenant is your ticket out of there. The following, would be one of many Scriptures to pray on. This is one of many Greater Exodus Scriptures:

For I know the plans I am planning for you, ' declares YHWH, 'plans of peace and not of evil, to give you an expectancy and a latter end.

'Then you shall call on Me, and shall come and pray to Me, and I shall listen to you.

'And you shall seek, and shall find Me, when you search for Me with all your heart.

'And I shall be found by you,' declares YHWH, and I SHALL TURN BACK YOUR CAPTIVITY, AND SHALL GATHER YOU FROM ALL THE GENTILES AND FROM ALL THE PLACES WHERE I HAVE DRIVEN YOU, DECLARES YHWH. AND I SHALL BRING YOU BACK TO THE PLACE FROM WHICH I HAVE EXILED YOU.' ''

- Jeremiah 29:11-14

But wasn't the Exodus in 1948, when they restored the country of Israel? Answer: that was the House of Judah (only two of the twelve tribes). Judah is only one of two sticks. The other ten tribes (the other stick) is known as Ephraim or Israel and consist of those who have been grafted in all over the world.

The kingdom was divided into Ephraim and Judah and both of them broke the covenant. However, as the following Scripture indicates; the kingdom is being restored by the joining of the two sticks.

And the word of YHWH came to me, saying,

''And you, son of man, take a stick for yourself and write on it, 'For Yahudah and for the children of Yisrael, his companions.' Then take another stick and write on it, 'For Yoseph, the stick of Ephrayim, and for all the house of Yisrael, his companions.'

''Then bring them together for yourself into one stick, and they shall become one in your hand.

''And when the children of your people speak to you, saying, 'Won't you show us what you mean by these?'

say to them, 'Thus said the Adonai YHWH, ''See, I am taking the stick of Yoseph, which is in the hand of Ephrayim, and the tribes of Yisrael, his companions. And I shall give them unto him, with the stick of Yahudah, and make them one stick, and they shall be one in my hands.'' '

''And the sticks on which you write shall be in your hand before their eyes.

''And speak to them, 'Thus said the Adonai YHWH, ''See, I am taking the children of Yisrael from among the gentiles, wherever they have gone, and shall gather them from all around, and I shall bring them into their own land.

''And I shall make them one nation in the land, on the mountains of Yisrael. And one sovereign shall be sovereign over them all, and let them no longer be two nations, and let them no longer be divided into two reigns.''

- Ezekiel 37:15-22

Answer the following questions:

1. If you want to know what happens at end you must

_____

_____

_____

2. Compare 1 Corinthians 10:1-12 to Ezekiel 20:34-36.
Describe how these passages of Scripture are similar to
each other.

_____

_____

_____

3. What happened in the 1st Exodus (or Egyptian Exodus)
to those who disobeyed the Torah?

_____

_____

_____

4. Explain why the future Exodus described in the given
Isaiah, Jeremiah, and Ezekiel Scriptures is not the
exodus from 1948.

_____

_____

_____

5. What do the "TWO STICKS" represent from Ezekiel
37:15-22?

_____

_____

_____

6. Read 2 Thessalonians 2:2-4. If the son of destruction (man of sin) is the anti-messiah and if the Great Tribulation begins after this anti-messiah's rebellious stand; does this disprove the theory of a pre-tribulation rapture?

_____

_____

_____

7. Explain why Jeremiah 29:11-14 describes YHWH's plan for the end of the age to save His people?

_____

_____

_____

8. Read Jeremiah 16:14-16 and Jeremiah 23:7-8 and explain how these two passages of Scripture are similiar to each other.

_____

_____

_____

9. In Jeremiah 16:16, What are the fishermen fishing and the hunters hunting? (Refer to Jeremiah 16:14-15 for the answer).

_____

_____

_____

10. Read 1 Corinthians 10:11-12 and explain why the people in the first exodus were examples for us - to whom the ends of the ages have come.

_____

_____

_____

11. What is the name of the camp where the first (Egyptian) exodus started?

_____

_____

_____

12. Why is The Feast of Tabernacle (Sukkot) a set-apart rehearsal for the Greater (or Next) Exodus?

_____

_____

_____

13. What is a booth?

_____

_____

_____

14. What is being described in Isaiah 4:5-6? Being that Isaiah was born and prophesied after the first exodus, what then is he describing?

_____

_____

_____

15. Why is it important to pray to be part of the Next Exodus? How does YHWH say He will respond if you do?

_____

_____

_____

Sabbath (Shabbat)

Our Engagement Ring

Exodus 31:13 states: You must keep my Sabbaths; for this is a sign between Me and you throughout the ages, that you may know that I, YHWH have consecrated you.

And so, Sabbath, from sundown Friday to sundown Saturday is the sign of our everlasting Covenant, the sign that we are children of the Most-High.

So, then a Sabbath rest still remains for the people of Elohim. -Hebrews 4:9

Shabbat means: "Rest," which is the central theme of this important observance. From ancient to modern times, humans have always needed proper rest and refreshment. In His infinite wisdom, Elohim told the children of Israel to recharge themselves physically, emotionally, and spiritually. He demonstrated this principle when He created the universe: for six days He formed the world and everything in it, but on the seventh day He rested. Consequently, the seventh day, Shabbat, is to be a perpetual reminder of Elohim the Creator and our need to find rest, not just in general but in Him as well (Exod. 31:16-17).

The weekly Sabbath has always been related to peace. Thus, the greeting "Shabbat Shalom" - Sabbath peace. The Sabbath of Millenia is described as the time of the Covenant of Peace (1,000 Year Reign) also known as the 7,000th year.

If you refrain from trampling the Sabbath, from pursuing your own interests on my set apart day, if you call the Sabbath a delight and the set apart day of YHWH honorable, if you honor it, not going your own way, serving your own interests or pursuing your own affairs, then you shall take delight in YHWH, and I make you ride on the heights of the earth, I will feed you with the heritage of your ancestor Ya'akov, for the mouth of YHWH has spoken - Isaiah 58:13-14

1. What does Shabbat Shalom mean?

_____

_____

_____

2. What is the central theme of Shabbat?

_____

_____

_____

3. When is the Sabbath of Millenia?

_____

_____

_____

4. What is Shabbat a perpetual reminder of?

_____

_____

_____

Saved by Grace

So, Moses went back and summoned the elders of the people and set before them all the words that YHWH had commanded him to speak. The people all responded together, "We will do everything that YHWH has said." So, Moses brought their answer back to YHWH.

- Exodus 19:7-8

Yeshua is the Bridegroom, we (the children of Abraham - saved by the Blood) are the Bride. Like any other marriage, we are married by Grace. We commit to any marriage with the promise that we will both fulfill our vows.

We cannot fulfill these vows (or Commandments) without Yeshua, nor should we try. He is the reason for the Vows, and only through the power of His Grace can we understand what the Vows mean.

In a marriage between a man and a woman; it may take years for both people to realize the commitment they have made.

Yeshua shows us through our relationship with Him that it should not just be legalism (or simply a legal contract). There must be love. Love fulfills the Law (or The Torah).

Let no debt remain outstanding, except the continuing debt to love another, for whoever loves others has fulfilled the Torah. The Commandments, "You shall not commit adultery," "You shall not murder," "You shall not steal," "You shall not covet," and whatever other command there may be, are summed up in this one command: "Love your neighbor as yourself." Love does no harm to a neighbor. Therefore, love is the fulfillment of the Torah."

- Romans 13:8-10

Grace picks us up and carries us when we fall short of keeping the Commandments (our wedding vows with Yeshua). Yeshua is the living word, the word in the flesh. Our Elohim is an Elohim of the living, not of the dead.

Paul never stopped confessing the wedding contract or his commitment to these vows.

I believe everything that is in accordance with the Torah and that is written in the Prophets.

- Acts 24:14

However, he was not foolish enough to believe that he could fulfill these vows without Yeshua and the power of Grace.

Then Paul made his defense: "I have done nothing wrong against the Jewish Law or against the temple or against Caesar." - Acts 25:8

These statements went over the heads of the Jewish leaders.

Some insist we must throw out the wedding vows. This is not consistent with the Scriptures:

The one who says he stays in Him ought to himself also to walk, even as He walked. - 1 John 1:6

If we love Him, we will do as He did. He followed the Commandments.

Everyone doing sin also does lawlessness, and sin is lawlessness. - 1 John 3:4

The English word "Lawlessness" here is taken from the Greek word "ANOMIA" which means "without the Torah." So, what this Scripture is essentially saying is: Everyone engaged in sin is without the Torah, and sin is not living by the Torah.

And by this we know that we know Him, if we guard His Commands. - 1 John 2:3

For this is the love for YHWH, that we guard His Commands, and His Commands are not heavy. - 1 John 5:3

"Do not think that I came to destroy the Torah or the Prophets. I did not come to destroy but to fulfill. For assuredly, I say to you, till heaven and earth pass away, one jot or one tittle will by no means pass from the Torah till all are fulfilled. Whoever therefore breaks one of the least of these commandments, and teaches men so, shall be called least in the kingdom of heaven but whoever does and teaches them, he shall be called great in the kingdom of heaven."

- Matthew 5:17-19

Always hold the Words of Yeshua in highest regard. His Words and His actions trump ALL other Words and actions.

Interestingly enough, Matthew 5:17-19 does not create confusion, it provides clarity (for those who are able to receive what it is saying). The Greek word translated as "fulfill" is PLEROSAI which means: to fill up, to fully preach, to make full, to make complete. It does not mean to destroy, dissolve, or demolish which is KATALOOSAI in the Greek.

What did He mean when He said: till the heavens and earth pass away? Clearly the heavens and earth have not yet passed away.

And I saw a renewed heavens and a renewed earth, for the former heavens and the former earth had passed away, and the sea is no more. - Revelation 21:1

John's vision here is what will be after the thousand-year reign. John saw the new heavens and new earth (8th day). What Yeshua is saying is that we are to observe the Torah until the Bride (New Jerusalem) is presented to our Eternal King Yeshua, on the 8th day (Eternal dimension). Remember the day that Israel said, "I do," we vowed to follow the Torah (wedding contract).

The word that Isaiah the son of Amos saw concerning Judah and Jerusalem: And it shall be in the latter days that the mountain of the House of YHWH is established on the top of the mountains and shall be exalted above the hills. And all the nations shall flow to it.

And many peoples shall come and say, 'Come, and let us go up to the mountain of YHWH, to the House of the Elohim of Ya'aqob, and let Him teach us in His Ways, and let us walk in His paths, for out of Zion comes forth the Torah, and the Word of YHWH from Jerusalem."

And He shall judge between the nations and shall reprove many peoples. And they shall beat their swords into ploughshares, and their spears into pruning hooks; nation shall not lift up sword against nation, neither teach battle anymore. - Isaiah 2:1-4

You see these same words in Micah 4:1-5. The prophecies are clear. They tell us that - in the latter days - the Renewed Covenant will involve the Torah being written on our hearts and in our minds and that the Messiah will rule according to the Torah. He will teach us the Torah from Zion.

Being "Saved by Grace" does not make the Torah obsolete.

1. What does the word ANOMIA mean? Why is it important?

_____

_____

_____

2. What are the two Scriptures given which describe Yeshua teaching the Torah from the Mount Zion? Will this be in the future?

_____

_____

_____

3. When will the Torah (or The Law) be fulfilled?

_____

_____

_____

4. Describe how one keeps their vows out of love. What is the difference between love and legalism?

_____

_____

_____

5. True or False. The Words and actions of the Messiah are our guide for what is pleasing to the Father. No one should ever trump the Messiah.

_____

_____

_____

Bereshith

The Book of Genesis

The Hebrew name for the First Book of Moses was originally Sever Maaseh Bereshith, "Book of Creation." This was rendered into Greek by Genesis, 'origin,' because it gives an account of the creation of the world and the beginnings of life and society. Its current Jewish name is Bereshith (In the beginning), which is the first Hebrew word in its opening sentence.

If the Pentateuch (which is a Greek word meaning the five books of Moses) were merely a code of civil and religious laws, it would have opened with the twelfth chapter of Exodus, which contains the earliest specific commandment given to Israel. But it is far more than a code of law: it is the Torah, i.e. the Divine Teaching given to Israel, and the Message of Israel to mankind. Therefore, it describes the origins of the Jewish people; traces its kinship to the other portions of the human family - all being of one blood and offspring of one common stock, and goes back to the creation of the world, which it declares to be the work of One Almighty and Beneficent Elohim. All this is told in the first eleven chapters of Genesis. The remaining thirty-nine chapters give the story of the Fathers of the Jewish people - Abraham, Isaac, Jacob and his children.

Origin of the Universe and the Beginnings of the Human Race

In the beginning

Verse 1 is a majestic summary of the story of Creation: Elohim is the beginning, the Cause of all things. The remainder of the chapter gives details of the successive acts of creation. Ages untold may have elapsed between the calling of matter into being and the reduction of chaos to ordered arrangement.

Elohim. Hebrew: ELOHIM

The existence of the Deity is throughout Scripture assured. It is not a matter for argument or doubt. ELOHIM is the general designation of the Divine Being in the Bible, as the fountain and source of all things. Elohim is a plural form, which is often used in Hebrew to denote plenitude of might (MIGHTY ONE). Here it indicates that Elohim comprehends and unifies all the forces of eternity and infinity.

Created

The Hebrew word is in the singular, thus precluding any idea that its subject, ELOHIM, is to be understood in a plural sense. The term is used exclusively of Divine activity. Man is spoken of as 'making' or 'forming,' but never as 'creating,' i.e. producing something out of nothing.

Hovered

The Hebrew word occurs again only in Deuteronomy 32:11, where it is descriptive of the eagle hovering over the young to care for them and protect them. Matter in itself is lifeless. The Spirit of Elohim quickens it and transforms it into material for a living world. The Jerusalem Targum translates this verse: 'And the earth was vacancy and desolation, solitary of the sons of men and void of every animal, and darkness was upon the face of the abyss.... and the Spirit of Mercies from before YHWH breathed upon the face of the waters.'

First Day. Creation of Light.

By the word of YHWH were the heavens made, Psalm 33:6. One of the names for Elohim in later Jewish literature is 'He who spoke and the world came into existence.' The phrase "Elohim said," must be taken as a figurative equivalent of "Elohim willed." Hence, His will is His word.

Let There Be Light

A sublimely simple phrase to express a sublime fact. This light, which is distinct from that radiated later on from the sun, disperse the darkness that enshrouded the Deep (verse 2). The old question, Whence did the light issue before the sun was made, is answered by the nebular theory! The great astronomer Halley wrote: "These nebulae reply fully to the difficulty which has been raised against the Mosaic description of creation, in asserting that light could not be generated without the sun."

In calling the light Day, Elohim defines the significance of light in human light. In the Bible account of Creation, everything centers around man and is viewed from his angle.

And There Was Evening

The day, according to the Scriptural reckoning of time, begins with the preceding evening. Thus, the observance of the Day of Atonement is to be 'from even unto even' (Leviticus 23:32), and similarly of the Sabbath and Festivals.

One Day

Not an ordinary day but a Day of Elohim, an age. With Him a thousand years, a thousand thousand ages, are but as a day that is past. Earthly and human measurement of time, by a clock of human manufacture, cannot apply to the first three days, as the sun was not then in existence. The beginning of each period of creation is called morning; it's close, evening. In the same way, we speak of the morning and evening of life.

Heaven

In the Bible, Heaven (shamayim) is represented as the habitation of Elohim, in the figurative sense in which the Temple is similarly described: 'Behold, heaven and the heaven of heavens cannot contain Thee: how much less this house I have builded! (1 Kings 8:27).

Earth Bring Forth

Elohim speaks to the source of what He wants it made out of. When He wanted fish, He spoke to the water. When He wanted plants, He spoke to the earth. When He created man, He was speaking to Himself. When He wanted a woman, He didn't go to the ground. He went to the man. He hides the end in the beginning. Every apple seed becomes an apple tree. Every boy becomes a man, every girl a woman. Every fish becomes a school. Every bird becomes a flock.

Man

Hebrew: Adam. The word is used here, as frequently in the Bible, in the sense of "human being." It is derived from ADAMAH 'earth,' to signify that man is earth-born.

In Our Image, After Our Likeness

Man is made in the 'image' and 'likeness' of Elohim: his character is potentially Divine. 'Elohim created man to be immortal and made him to be an image of His own eternity' (Wisdom of Solomon 2:23). Man alone among living creatures is gifted, like His Creator, with moral freedom and will. He is capable of knowing and loving Elohim, and of holding spiritual communion with Him; and man alone can guide his actions in accordance with Reason. 'On this account he is said to have been made in the form and likeness of the Almighty. Because man is endowed with Reason, he can subdue his impulses in the service of moral and religious ideals and is born to bear rule over nature. Psalm 8 says of man: 'O YHWH, Thou hast made him but little lower than the angels, and hast crowned him with glory and honour. Thou hast made him to have dominion over the works of Thy hands.'

Sabbath

Note carefully how Elohim goes about His work in forming and filling: He separates. One of the first acts we find Elohim doing is separating - making a distinction between light and dark. Our havdalah service (the word HAVDALAH comes from the very Hebrew word BADAL used in Genesis 1 and translated "separate") to emphasize this separation - the need to separate between things that differ, and ultimately between the holy and the profane. Elohim is a Elohim of distinction - He does not mix things that essentially differ. As those who want to emulate the righteousness of Elohim, we must also be willing to make distinctions - to separate between those things that please Him and those things which do not.

Not only does Elohim separate within the physical universe, but He also separates in the sphere of time: the six days of creation are separated from the seventh day of rest. While the work carried out on the six days of creation is all stated to be "good" (a phrase found twice on the 3rd day, which is why the Sages considered the 3rd day especially propitious for a wedding), no day is blessed except the Sabbath - the seventh day: "And Elohim blessed the seventh day and set it apart:" (2:3). What is the meaning of blessing a day? It is possible that we should understand the text to mean: "Elohim blessed the Sabbath by setting apart," that is, He gave special honor to the Sabbath by separating it from the other days of work. Or could it mean that in blessing the seventh day Elohim intended us to know that in some way that day would bring a blessing. Both are no doubt true. A well known saying: "it is not so much that Israel has kept the Sabbath, as that the Sabbath has kept Israel." This day of rest, initiated by Elohim Himself, and a foreshadow and revelation of the rest that mankind would have in Elohim's mercy and redemption, would become the very sign of the covenant made between Elohim and His people Israel (Exodus 31). Thus, the creation as described in Genesis 1 looks forward to the covenant that Elohim would make with His people. Once again, the focus is not upon the physical creation, but upon the plan of Elohim to dwell among His people. The world was created as the platform for Elohim's drama of redemption, and thus the Sabbath, set apart from the beginning, becomes the covenant sign between Elohim and Israel.

The Sabbath is Elohim's gift to His friends. In the physical world the times and season are clearly marked by the sun and moon. Even if one had no modern timepiece, he could calculate the month (by the moon) and the year (by the sun). But one simply cannot find a week etched into the time frame of the universe. If one were alone on an island, one could determine the span of a day, a month, and a year, but one could never know what day of the week it was simply by observing the created world. No, the week with its ordered days, and the Sabbath as the week's completion, is the gift of Elohim to His own children. And thus, in this way, it is blessed and set apart. Only through the gracious revelation of Elohim is the Sabbath known.

And what does the Sabbath teach us? That there is rest indeed if one knows Elohim. There is a promised place of solitude, of refreshing, of companionship if one knows Elohim. But only if one takes Elohim at His word, and strives to pattern one's life after the very Elohim Who created - only then is the gift of Sabbath enjoyed. For ultimately the Sabbath (like all of the appointed times) points to Elohim's Messiah, Yeshua. In Him we find our rest, for only in Him is there forgiveness of sins. In all of our striving, and all of our efforts, we never can rid ourselves of the penalty of sin, that is death. But in Yeshua there is life, for by His sacrifice we are redeemed and brought back to Eden where we can be restored to our creative purpose: friendship with Elohim. Thus, in Yeshua we rest - we cease our striving, and by faith we anticipate the fulfillment of the covenant when time will be no more, and the eternal Sabbath will be ushered in.

Works Cited

Resources for Broken Road Ministries:

Yahweh's Evangelical Assembly

PO BOX 31

Atlantic, TX 75551

The House of Yahweh

PO BOX 2498

Abilene, TX 79604

Assemblies of Yahweh

PO BOX C

Bethel, PA 19507

Yahweh's Assembly in Messiah

401 N Roby Farm Rd

Rocheport, MO 65279

Todd Bennett's - Walk in the Light Series- available on
www.shemayisrael.net

Halleluyah Scriptures

PO BOX 2283

Vineland, NJ 08362-2283

Bradford Scott- wildbranch.org

74

Joel Richardson- The Islamic Antichrist

Rabbi Jonathan Cahn- www.hopeoftheworld.org

Michael Rood- www.rooadawakening.tv

Monte Judah- www.lionandlambministries.org

Eddie Chumney- www.eddiechumney.com

Hebraic Heritage Ministries International - hebroots.org

Studies in the Torah by Tim Hegg

The Laws of the Second Coming by Dr. Stephen Jones

What is available to me from Broken Road Ministries?

The Torah Study Series Volumes 1 to 8. These are the books in order:

Volume 1

This is where it all starts. The Basics. This book explains what the Torah is. It teaches about the Sabbath. It contains several chapters: We wrestle not against flesh and blood, The measure you use, who is your neighbor, Bereshith (an-in depth analysis of the Hebrew in the book of Genesis).

Volume 2

This book teaches the Moadim (Appointed Times from Leviticus 23). Contains the following chapters: Passover (Pesach), Feast of Unleavened Bread - Khag Ha'Matzah, Shavuot - Feast of Weeks, Passover and the Feast of Unleavened Bread, The Number Seven, The Counting of the Omer, Foot Washings, Yom Teruah - Feast of Trumpets, Ten Days of Awe, Yom Kippur - Day of Atonement, The 7th Day, Feast of Tabernacles (Sukkot), Shemini Atzeret - The 8th Day of Ingathering, Purim, Shemot (Exodus 1:1-6:1), Israel's Prophetic Spring Feasts, and a Multiple-choice Exam at the end of the book.

Volume 3

The Name (HaShem) - Is it YHWH or Yehovah? This is a compelling Bible Study which may help you if you are in pursuit of a conclusive answer.

Elohim's Servants Scourged - Will there be scourging at The White Throne Judgment. BRM takes a look at this predominantly Christian teaching.

Volume 4

Contains Torah portion studies from the Book of Exodus.

Volume 5

Contains the following chapters: Foreword 2022, Remembering Our Redemption (Exodus 13:1-20), Lessons from Pesach (Exodus 12:13-28), Jacob's Feast Day Pattern, Bo (Exodus 12:29-51), The Feast Days in the Book of Joel, B' SHALACH "When He Sent" (Exodus 13:21-15:18), The 7,000 Year Plan of Elohim, The Messiah Part 2, The Feast Days in Elijah's Story, Renewal.

Volume 6

Contains Bible studies from Torah portions in Genesis, Exodus, and Leviticus.

Volume 7

Contains the following chapters: The Blood Cries Out, TSAV "Command" Leviticus 8:1-36/Hebrews 7:11-28, Presenting the Firstborn, MISHPATIM "Ordinances" Exodus 21:1-22:24, Two or Three Witnesses, BEMIDBAR "In the Desert" (Numbers 1:1-2:13), Elohim's Face is Elohim's Presence, Resist Babylon.

Volume 8

This is a book which stands against racism/antisemitism.

We all know that this picture of a milky white "Jesus" that we inherited from the Puritans of England is not an accurate depiction of Yeshua, our Messiah (simply because of where in the world He was born!)

Perhaps Yeshua was not as black as portrayed on the cover of this book. However, it serves to make a point. Why the fear of a darker skin color on our Messiah? Why the need to change His Name? What is going on here?

I knew I had to put this book together, after a rather disturbing trip to the chapel one day at an institution. At a Christian service, there broke out a question-and-answer portion to the service. A (black) man stood up (politely) and asked, "Isn't His Name really Yeshua?" The (white) speaker (a volunteer who comes in once a week) with all sincerity responded "No, His Name is Jesus."

Something is wrong with this.

We are going to explore where this DISCONNECT started; all the way back to the pioneers of Christianity (as it broke off from the Roman Catholic Church).

Siddur

Prayer Journal

For a free copy of any of these books write to:

Broken Road Ministries

P.O. Box 780751

Orlando, FL 32878

Made in United States
Troutdale, OR
08/05/2024

21751939R00044